# What does your dog really want to eat?

## THE COMPLETE "COOK" BOOK FOR YOUR DOG

# What does your dog really want to eat?

## THE COMPLETE "COOK" BOOK FOR YOUR DOG

*by* **William Campbell Douglass II,** MD

Rhino Publishing, S.A.
www.RhinoPublish.com
Republic of Panama

# What does your dog really want to eat?

## THE COMPLETE "COOK" BOOK FOR YOUR DOG

This edition is published by Rhino Publishing.
For information, contact **Christian Martin Desharnais**
through Rhino Publishing website, www.RhinoPublish.com

Published in the Republic of Panama.

ISBN: 978-9962-636-81-6

Book designed by Lourdes Jaramillo (lourja@cwpanama.net)

Please, visit Rhino's website for other publications from
Dr. William Campbell Douglass
**www.rhinopublish.com**
RHINO PUBLISHING, S.A.
World Trade Center
Panama, 00832-2483
Republic of Panama

*To Ian Billinghurst, DVM...*
*The pioneer in returning our pets*
*to a normal diet*
*and a healthy long life*

# Acknowledgements:

My heartfelt thanks to Laurie Mathena and all the other "worker bee" ladies at AGORA Publishing to whom I owe so much of my success. And a mention of thanks to my publisher, Christian Martin Desharnais, of Rhino Publishing, without whose encouragement my previous books would not have survived and the new ones would not have been written.

# CONTENTS

# What does your dog really want to eat?

## THE COMPLETE "COOK" BOOK FOR YOUR DOG

The answer to the title of this book, "What Does Your Dog Really Want to Eat?" is really quite simple. I am going to answer the question in 50 pages or less. And please note that "cook" is in parentheses as *there is no cooking at all*.

The pet holocaust we have experienced recently was unimaginable to most pet owners. Yet, we have been railing at the junk pet food industry for years and warning pet owners that these "kibble companies" were destroying the health of their furry friends; few listened. Remember that these admonitions to you were given long before the melamine mass poisoning took place and <u>never would have happen if you had been feeding your dog properly.</u>

*It was not your fault*; how would you have known (unless you were a regular reader of the Douglass Report) that most of the advice the junk pet food industry was promulgating was false and inimical to the health of your beloved friend?

The worst example of this false and damaging information, which led to millions of heart attacks, diabetes, obesity and arthritis – especially in dogs – came from Petco. It was so gross that it is hard to imagine any qualified veterinarian having approved of it. I am reprinting it here from a 2006 issue of the *Douglass Report.*

## Nutritional propaganda from PETCO could mean big problems for your pet

If you're into pampering your pet, PETCO undoubtedly has the product for you. Apparently, they have all the luxuries you and your dog or cat could hope for—everything from thrones and booties to medical insurance.

But when it comes to nutrition, they're out to lunch. Their advice is outrageous, dangerous, and abysmally ignorant all rolled into one ridiculous package. I found it hard to believe a company of this size (over 650 stores) could be so wrong and basically anti-nutrition. But, come to think of it, why would I think that? It's not like General Foods and Kellogg's give sound nutritional advice for *people*—why should PETCO for—*animals*?

According to the PETCO website, "some foods must never be fed to dogs because they may produce symptoms ranging from indisposition to illness to death. These include chocolate, onions, raw eggs and meats, liver, bones, pork..."

Any pet owner with an IQ equal to his dog would know not to feed chocolate to the animal. (By the way, how much toxic chocolate candy do you feed to your children? Don't they deserve a good diet too?) But chocolate is not the same as chocolate candy. That's another story.

The liver warning is based on complete nonsense. I wrote about the liver toxicity myth 20 years ago. There had been stories circulation for years, dating back to the 18th and 19th centuries about explorers getting sick and even dying from eating too much polar bear liver. Investigation revealed <u>not one such case</u> in the medical literature. But PETCO must still be living in the 18th century, since they're still worried that "if your dog eats raw liver or consumes three servings of cooked liver a week, he could be headed for problems..." and PETCO tells their customers: "Also, always cook liver; never feed it raw." This is absolute nonsense. And as for raw eggs and bones...?

What does your dog love most? -- **A _bone_**. But PETCO, looking at the cash register, I suspect, tells their clients: "The big, treated bones that you can buy your pet in a pet store are of an entirely different composition from the bones and the meat you buy at the grocery. Store-bought bones are specially treated so that they will not splinter." What a joke. A few months ago, I bought one of these splinter-free, vacuum-wrapped bones at the pet store for $3.50 (the big ones are $10). I put it in the cupboard and planned to give it to my dog Silky, a 16-week-old Weimaraner, to see if she liked it at all. A week later I opened the cupboard to find that the bone was swarming with red ants—even though it had been protected with vacuum wrap. The thing was undoubtedly loaded with sugar.

Maybe that's how they "treat" the bones so they won't splinter, but that's certainly no way to treat your dog. I'll tell you how to "treat" a nice knee-joint bone for your dog: Buy it at the butcher shop; take it home; unwrap the package; throw it on the garage floor and let the fun begin. It will cost you little and, if you are a steady customer, the butcher may <u>give</u> it to you. Splintering only occurs when the bone has been cooked and dried out. If you leave it raw, it won't cause any problems. The "problem" will only be that Jake or Jane will insist of one joint a day.

## Raw eggs don't equal rotten eggs

Once PETCO finished attacking bones, they moved onto another favorite canine treat: eggs. Did you know that you're going to give your precious pet a <u>biotin deficiency</u> with consequent hair loss, weakness and growth retardation if you feed him raw eggs? At least, those are the red flags PETCO is waving about raw eggs.

"Although athletes seem constantly to be consuming raw eggs in one variety or another," they say, "think twice before giving your pet raw eggs. Although cooked eggs are high in protein and make an excellent treat, raw egg whites contain a protein called avidin, which can deplete your dog of biotin, one of the B vitamins. Biotin is essential to your dog's growth and coat health."

Right. "Think twice" and then give your pup <u>plenty</u> of raw eggs. He (like you) could live well on nothing but raw eggs. Let me explain: The complete raw egg is a perfectly <u>balanced food</u>, like some of our other natural foods. The yolk of the egg neutralizes the avidin so it is a non-issue. If you (or your pet) were to eat large quantities of egg white without the yolk, you <u>might</u> get a biotin deficiency. But even that is unlikely, unless you feed him (or yourself) lemon meringue pie three times a day. So do you see how these crooks are manipulating your mind?

"Additionally," they advise, "raw eggs are often contaminated with bacteria, such as salmonella, and you could end up giving your dog food poisoning in addition to biotin deficiency." Wrong again. A dog will eat practically"<u>anything</u> including paper, rotten meat or fruit, tree bark, bugs, and feces. I know you don't like to hear that about your little Fido, but it is true. Spend a week on a farm; watch the free and happy dogs at play and you will see what I mean. And yet, none of these scavengers seem to have a problem with food poisoning. That's because animals are remarkably resistant to intestinal infection – if they are fed only *real* dog food i.e. raw animal fat and raw animal protein – fresh or rotten.

Your dog probably <u>is</u> finicky, but that's because what he eats is all he knows. Fido will probably turn up his cute little nose at raw chicken liver because  he has become civilized and doesn't know that chicken liver is the very best food he could eat—and that's the way PETCO likes it.

## The three foods PETCO <u>does</u> allow — and why your dog shouldn't eat them

**According to PETCO,** "there are three basic types of food: dry, semi-moist, and canned." Notice there's <u>no mention</u> of fresh meat or animal organs. Fresh raw meat, raw eggs, raw liver, raw chicken necks, and bones <u>do not exist</u>. You'd think, the way PETCO sees the world, that all dogs cooked their food in the wild. "Raw" is a dirty word and is mentioned only to tell you how raw animal food is dangerous to your pet's health — and, of course, let's not forget how troublesome it can be for PETCO's bottom line.

Here's what they have to say about the kinds of food they do acknowledge:

<u>Dry Food</u>: "It's the most economical choice. Dry food isn't smelly, can be stashed anywhere, and won't spoil if it sits in your dog's dish all day." Note the pitch is <u>for the convenience of the owner</u>, not the pet. And the food doesn't spoil because it is completely unnatural and nutrition-free.

<u>Semi-moist Food</u>: "Like dry food, semi-moist food doesn't need to be refrigerated, so it's easy to use and store."

<u>Canned Food:</u> "Our canine friends pick canned food paws down." But, PETCO

warns: "Canned food also spoils quickly once it's been opened, so you can't leave it out all day." Hmmm...it must have <u>some</u> food value left then. But it is still cooked, mostly vegetable food that is unfit for man or beast.

They blather on about the varying quality of chow available—generic, name brand grocery, premium, etc., but make no mention of the stuff—from the butcher counter that your pet longs to eat. And there's a not-so-subtle condemnation of the grocery store bags as compared to <u>their</u> bags: "Ingredients in individual generic brands vary from bag to bag, which could upset your pal's stomach. Manufacturers will use the cheapest ingredients available to them at the time the food is produced so different batches of the same brand will have different ingredients, and abrupt changes in your dog's diet might throw his digestive system off." But it *doesn't matter* (I'm going to continue saying this until you're sick and tired of hearing it) because it's still cooked, vegetarian food.

"At some point, your dog also may develop such health problems as kidney or heart disease, which require premium foods that are developed specifically to help manage these conditions. Your veterinarian will advise you if your dog needs a premium therapeutic food."

They are just a manipulation of the same old grit. The Pet food industry realizes that if your beloved friend is seriously ill, you'll pay almost any amount to get him well. But the reason your dog gets "heart or kidney disease"—*and* diabetes, obesity, arthritis, and cancer – is because you followed their nutrition advice in the first place.

I can guarantee you your dog will develop "such health problems as kidney or heart disease" if you continue to feed him a diet of meatless kibble. They may call it "real beef," "real fish," or "real chicken," but it isn't any more real than a nutrient-fortified Oreo cookie. Keep in mind that "meat by-product" does not mean meat. Paper is a byproduct of trees but paper is not a tree. And beware of the "therapeutic" or "premium" label. It's just more of the same vegetarian crapola.

The bottom line in all this? Well, how can I express it delicately? As we say in Central America: "Senor PETCO, "ignorance overflows from your pores." You are a fraud and you are corrupting American dogdom and catdom with very bad nutritional advice. You are selling nothing more than <u>expensive junk food</u> and setting our pets up for diabetes, obesity, heart disease, arthritis and cancer.

Father Nature must be rolling in his grave.

PETCO—not raw food—is a clear and present danger to your pet. My dogs, Silky and Hannibal get <u>raw</u> liver twice weekly, and a <u>raw</u> egg daily mixed in with the shell, and <u>raw</u> chicken necks—no cooked food at all, except for occasional table scraps that fall to the floor. With this diet, you will have the top dog on your block—guaranteed.

Caveat: The table scraps that "accidentally" fall to the floor, are usually not fit for homo sapiens or beast. <u>Don't spoil your pets with human food</u>.

Petco is also an authority on animal psychology and exercise physiology. These next few paragraphs are so inane, childish and insulting to your intelligence that I am going to summarize them for you. I don't want you to break a rib laughing.

"Dogs can suffer from the same types of obesity-related illnesses as people, so establishing a physical fitness routine from the start is not only good for your pup, but can help you achieve your fitness goals, too. Plus, a good exercise plan for your puppy enhances good physical development and can help avoid arthritis and other joint-related problems later in life," Petco says.

Did you know you need to devise an exercise plan for your puppy"—"puppy workouts"? This "physical fitness routine" will not only help avoid arthritis and other joint-related problems later in life, but it will also decrease "boredom behaviors like chewing and digging."

Well, you get the idea. Our recommendation for your puppy's physical fitness: Put him in your fenced back yard, preferably with another dog, and go back to your reading. If you don't have a'back yard, take him for a walk in the park.

A reminder: *Exercise will not prevent obesity*. (Perhaps you have learned that the hard way.) This is a complicated issue and it would require an entire book to explain it. However, a book has been written and the title is *The Exercise Myth by Dr. Henry Soloman, ISBN 0151294585*. The book is not easy to find but you can usually find copies on

Amazon.com. If you are lucky enough to find a copy, read it and then read it to your dog as he probably can't read. (No offense intended. My dog can't read either; in fact he not only doesn't read books, he <u>eats</u> books.)

**Reference: "Care sheets/Pet info: Dangerous foods,"**
**PETCO (<u>www.PETCO.com</u>)**

# KILLING OUR PETS FOLLOWED UP BY BAD ADVICE

With the tsunami of horrible news of the mass poisoning of our pets has come a second wave of <u>bad advice</u> from amateurs and nutritional experts of all varieties including veterinarians and university PhDs. I am sure you heard about the Chinese wheat gluten that was contaminated by a toxin and is believed to be the source of this tragedy. But did you hear that scientists at Cornell University found the rat poison, aminopterin, in samples of the recalled products? Aminopterin is a deadly toxin and suppresses the immune system (CBS News, March 23, 2007). So there are two suspected toxins in the Chinese wheat gluten, one from fertilizer and one from the rat poison.

According to the USDA, we imported <u>28 million pounds</u> of wheat gluten in 2006 from Communist China. One U.S. importer, the President of MGP, said their tests of Chinese gluten found it to be a "typically lower quality product" than those imported from First World companies (USA TODAY, March 24 2007).

So we have set the stage. What has been the response of our veterinary experts, university PhDs, government bureaucrats and the uneducated, largely irresponsible "free press"?

The Associated Press tells us: "But veterinarians warn that making balanced meals for pets can be complicated and should only be a temporary remedy until the scare passes." ***The "scare"?*** Hundreds, and possibly thousands of our pets are dead or dying and yet "veterinarians" (unnamed) are calling it a "scare"? The problem is that vets have been"completely taken in by the pseudo science of the pet food industry. The vets are perked and petted just like the pharmaceutical industry perks and pets the doctors of humans. There are, in both cases, reasons for going along for prestige and financial gain. "Making balanced meals" for dogs and cats is not complicated. They only need raw meat and raw animal fat —nothing else for a "balanced" diet. It's that simple. My two cats, Paint and Pistol, never had a thing to eat but raw chicken liver during their entire lives. They were never sick. They never went to a vet. They enjoyed their repast and ate it with enthusiasm.

"The veterinarian group also warned that many common foods are not safe for pets, including salt, garlic, onions, raisins, and chocolate. Now that is good advice but they should have added to their restricted list boiled potatoes, pasta, sugar and all commercial pet food, wet or dry.

The FDA and the American Veterinary Medical Association, AP reports, are urging pet owners to switch brands if they are worried (CBC News, April 4, 2007). "Switching brands" from one commercial pet food to another does not get to the heart of the problem. They are all bad – cooked, laden with fake grain protein (gluten), and almost always soy bean extracts that are not really food at all. Would switching from Coca Cola to Pepsi improve your health?

One concerned pet owner said to the AP reporter that he had abandoned all commercial pet foods and was making his own dinner for his two dogs: ground beef, boiled potatoes, and pasta. Why would you want to give boiled potatoes and pasta to dogs? Since it was described as a stew, the hamburger was cooked as well. So pet owner John, though meaning well, ended up with a concoction no better than the commercial ones he was serving before "the scare."

Making pet food at home is "kind of like canning: You have to think about bacterial contamination. And how do you make sure it's nutritionally appropriate and balanced for the animal?" said FDA spokeswoman Julie Zawisza to AP. She added: "We wouldn't object. We'd say be knowledgeable about what you need." (CBC News, April 4, 2007). Well, Julie, you could be a little more knowledgeable yourself. "Nutritionally appropriate and balanced" is <u>pet food factory propaganda</u> to convince professionals, like FDA spokeswomen, university nutritionists and veterinarians that their pet food industry serves an important need; that is, to determine the arcane and "complicated" science of cat and dog nutritional biochemistry. In actuality, factory food is a <u>serious public health problem</u> for our pets – and–for those people on the street who are forced to eat dog food because their job has been outsourced to China.

And it's not "kind of like canning." Appropriate food preparation for dogs and cats is <u>not canning</u> which requires <u>destructive heating</u>; it's raw animal food i.e. the flesh of <u>other animals</u> they need – fish, fowl and mammal.

Back in the 70s, when my Doberman, Greta, gave birth I had a delightful manger prepared for her in the garage. She had the puppies there only because she couldn't get out. She chewed off each of the nine umbilical cords as she delivered the pups, licked them clean and ate some of the placenta. The minute we left her in peace she took each one by the head and carried it into the woods where she had already prepared a nest to her liking. Your pet knows what it wants and needs but they are prisoners of their loving and sincere owners and the owners are prisoners of the tragically-flawed nutrition paradigm of the giant pet-food industry, which is basically a vegetarian diet with "meat flavors."

Ms. Zawisza remarked that you "have to think about bacterial contamination." I hate to pick on the FDA's spokeswoman but I cannot let the remark about bacterial contamination go unnoticed. Do modern vets, their university nutrition teachers, and medical bureaucrats ever go out into the countryside, or in the back alleys of the cities for that matter, and observe the secret life of dogs and cats? They are highly resistant to bacterial infection, especially of the intestinal tract, IF they have been raised on the proper raw diet.

They love rotten fruit, rotten vegetables and rotten meat. They delight in rolling in the poop of other animals; lick their butts and other dogs' butts. (Sorry for this repulsive elucidation of the secret life of your pets but its time you came out of the laboratory and your immaculate kitchen to learn what your pet really wants – fresh (or rotten), raw animal tissue – the bones, the blood, the fat, the liver, the whole disgusting mess).

On Amazon.com, the cookbook "Real Food for Dogs" moved into the list of top 200 best-sellers after the pet food disaster developed. Other authors were finding instant success, too. This book, *Real Food for Dogs,* has made a colossal accent into the heavens – into the top 200! (MSNBC April 3, 2007). That means, in economic terms, a million books or more sold. The authors got rich over night! As usual, only the public is swindled. The book is delightfully-written trash. The authors like 99 percent of the public, want to anthropomorphize your pets – if it's OK for you then it is OK for your dog or cat. In summary: the book is about <u>cooked food</u>, not "real food," and will guarantee your dog a sickly existence.

Dr Donald Strombeck is a retired professor of veterinary nutrition at the University of

California, Davis. His book, "Home-Prepared Dog & Cat Diets" has jumped from a 60,000 rank to a 1,000 rank. Yikes, another overnight millionaire! – and based on bad advice. His niche is, if the table food you eat is OK for you then the scraps are OK for your dog or cat. Well, the food you eat is <u>not</u> good for your pet because it is <u>cooked</u>. Dr Strombeck goes into the treatment of human diseases that have become animal diseases for the very reason that the cooked food they are eating is what <u>you</u> eat. Dr Strombeck's reasoning would be OK for the 1950s when he started his practice because 50 years ago we were still a rural nation and dogs and cats spent most of their time outside where they could supplement their table scraps with <u>real food</u> – raw animal tissue. His book is not recommended.

Robert Van Sickle, co-owner of the Polka Dog Bakery in Boston, said he has received many inquiries from customers on advice for making their own dog food. For his German short-haired pointer, Van Sickle blends carrots, spinach, salmon oil, apple cider vinegar and whatever meat is in his freezer. Well, at least the last item of advice is good; you can leave out the rest. But the salmon oil or cod liver oil is a good daily supplement for any mammal, including you. All the mammals in the Douglass household –myself included– get a cod liver oil capsule every day. I take it with water. Who wants to bite in to a capsule of cod liver oil? – YUK. But the doggies *love* them and eat them like candy. So you see? We really are different from our pets.

The only mammalian nutrition and "cookbook" (other than the one you are reading, of course) that I can recommend to you is published in Australia but now available in the U.S. at: www.barfworld.com. It is an excellent book. Every dog and cat should own a copy.

You can find the Barf Diet book on www.barfworld.com in their 'Books' section, (they primarily sell lots of frozen raw meat for pets), or, get it directly from www.barfaustralia.com.au.

E-mail: barfdiet@ix.net.au (More on "Dr BARF (BIOLOGICALLY APPROPRIATE FOODS)" at the end of the book.

## THE IRONY OF IT

I have written the pathetic story of doughy dogs and corpulent cats. If you are new to these pages, just let me say that turning our dogs and cats into vegetarians, which has led to pets as fat as their masters, is one of the great nutritional con jobs of the century, compliments of your vet and the pet food industry.

And recent news reveals the irony of this sorry spectacle. If you have ever watched dogs in their natural state, that is, free of can or dried dog/cat "food," you know they will eat practically anything that walks, crawls, slithers or flies —dead or alive. We could get down and dirty here and tell you some of the awful (to us) things they routinely eat if given a chance. They can eat the filthiest stuff with impunity – God is a dog lover, no doubt about it. But unless you were born and raised in a condo, never touch the ground, and never get your shoes dirty, much less your feet, you have an idea that dogs really are animals.

But in spite of this built-in resistance to eating practically anything, a pet food company in Texas has managed to make a pet food so bad that it has caused an epidemic of hepatitis, killing at least six dogs. The product, "Go! Natural," is produced by the Canadian company, *Petcurean Pet Nutrition*. Whether you are talking about human nutrition or pet nutrition, the word, "natural" is now meaningless except to tell you that the product is probably not natural.

## The Pet Food Disaster – Tip of the Iceberg

In mid-2007, I reported on the breaking story of contamination in mass-produced pet foods that has so far sickened and killed thousands of our beloved American pets — dog and cats, specifically. And because it was so early on in the crisis, I had very little information to impart to you about exactly what was causing these casualties.

But I did have some recommendations on how to safeguard your kitties and pups against this fate: To feed them ONLY raw liver, chicken necks, hamburger and any other uncooked meats and animal organs. (Yes, I am repeating myself.) This should include at least one daily raw egg — including the shell — rounding out their diet with cut vegetables put on top. (They always eat the vegetables last, if at all. But avocado they will always eat right along with the raw hamburger. I don't know why; you'll have to ask them.)

This advice directly contradicts not only everything you'll hear down at your local PetSmart store (or Petco, whatever), but also what several mainstream books recently published in wide release have to say about canine and feline diets, as mentioned above.

Today, there's even more proof of this. More information has surfaced about exactly WHY our precious pets are dying. And as usual when it comes to nutrition — human or animal— one thing lies at the root of all the evil...

## Vegetarianism

In case you haven't heard, the U.S. FDA is all but certain the source of the contamination that's sickening and killing our cats and dogs is melamine, a toxic chemical used in the manufacture of plastics, pesticides, and as a fertilizer. I mentioned this earlier. Melamine is high in nitrogen. Now *stay with me; this is the heart of the problem.*

Though deemed safe in low concentrations — as what might be found in vegetables grown in fields fertilized or insect-controlled with melamine — <u>direct ingestion</u> of the substance can be deadly. Yet according to the FDA, melamine poisoning is likely what's sickening and killing so many of our pets. This kind of contamination would be VERY DIFFICULT without somebody adding melamine directly to pet foods, or to their ingredients.

Why would anyone do this?

Despite the fact that it's nutritionally-insufficient for pets, all brands of modern pet foods — especially the dry varieties — are made almost entirely of vegetable ingredients. There are several reasons for this, foremost among them being cost. It's far cheaper to make pet foods from "soy this" and "wheat gluten that" than it is to use real meat (which is impossible in the dry foods anyway).

But since the average pet owner is at least aware of the fact that animals, like people, need PROTEIN to survive, pet food makers are big on adding things to their food to boost the *appearance of added nutrition*. And in this case, that "additive" was very likely poisonous melamine.

Remember I said before that nitrogen was the key here? According to a recent USA Today article, the agricultural industry typically gauges a raw grain's protein content by measuring its nitrogen content. Nitrogen levels generally correspond quite closely with protein levels...

Is the scam coming into focus?

You've got it — the FDA suspects that nitrogen-rich melamine fertilizer was added in raw form to large quantities of wheat and rice earmarked for pet foods in order to create the illusion that these worthless grains were higher in protein than they actually are. And please note this is <u>vegetable</u> protein, not <u>animal</u> protein which is what your pets require.

But this is only part of the story.

To sell more pet food, pet owners were deceived into believing the dry vegetable junk food they're feeding their cats and dogs is protein-rich and good for them (it's actually bad for them, melamine-laced or not). As this crisis has unfolded, more information about how this toxic stuff may have gotten into the foods has surfaced...

And it doesn't look good for the pet-food industry, or its retailers — your local super market or your own vet.

As it turns out, like everything else in this country nowadays, the raw ingredients for ALL of the banned varieties of pet foods came <u>not</u> from hard-working American grain farmers — whose products and harvesting practices are strictly regulated by the USDA, FDA, and other agencies...

They come from communist China, where pollution and environmental waste is rampant, regulation scarce, and where the jack-booted government values nothing (not even life) so much as the influx of American dollars. And that river of money is enhanced if Chinese raw grains are thought to be richer in protein than grains from other places — including the U.S.A.

According to FDA sources (their Chief Veterinarian, for one), <u>raw melamine</u> has been found — not just in the U.S, but in other nations, too — in rice protein concentrate, wheat gluten, and corn gluten supplies earmarked specifically for pet foods. All of these tainted stockpiles were imported from China.

Now, we might have been alerted to this sooner if the FDA was able to monitor more of the foodstuffs we import. According to the AP and CBS, the agency can only test 1% of the food or raw ingredients that cross our borders. I guess their budget is stretched too thin from testing all those drugs — because they're SO good at that, right? But that's another story... Of course, U.S. regulators can't PROVE that the Chi-comms are lacing Fido's food with melamine without inspecting the Chinese plants and farms themselves. And so far, that invitation hasn't been forthcoming. What HAS been coming out of China (besides killer grains and lethal lead laced toys) is a lot of double-talk and denials.

Silent after the first few weeks of the scandal, China is finally acknowledging that shipments of gluten and other food ingredients tainted with melamine originated on their shores. They've also instituted a new ban on the chemical from all food products they export...

But of course, China is rejecting melamine as a cause for any pets' deaths.

China's Foreign Ministry is also claiming that the tainted supplies slipped through their "normally rigorous customs inspections" because they were destined to be used as pet food. Yeah, I'm so sure — according to the AP/CBS piece, Chinese farmers have a well-documented history of exporting food products contaminated with human waste (ugh) and pesticides that are banned in the U.S., and other problems.

Aside from this, FDA investigators are getting the runaround from the Chinese. One of the 3 exporting companies the agency is focusing on claims that food ingredients aren't even part of its core business'— but that employees often make side deals to buy, sell and export such items.

All this brings up an interesting point: Do the prestigious retail companies (PetSmart, Petco, etc.) that represent themselves as knowing all about how to raise healthy pets actually even know the least bit about what kinds of foods they're selling — or where they come from? Think about it for a minute...

If they knew they were buying foods made by companies who bought their likely-contaminated raw ingredients from unregulated sources in shady, off-the-books back room deals — yet sold these foods anyway — what does that say about their scruples?

And if they DIDN'T know about all this, what does that say about their level of expertise in helping your pet lead a long and healthy life?

On the one hand, they're heartless criminal killers — and on the other, clueless dunces.

But again, there are still more layers to this "onion" of a story. Like how the risks of melamine-contaminated pet food aren't limited to Fido, but perhaps *have spread to the one who holds his leash.*

I have now brought you up to speed on the sordid saga behind the plight of pets here in the U.S. — at least those whose owners don't know to ignore the advice of vets and pet-store employees when it comes to your cats' and dogs' diets. (Yes, tragically, most of the vets have gone on the vegetarian bandwagon and many sell this trash food from their offices —"Doctor-recommended," you know.) As I've said repeatedly, the ONLY foods your little kittens and pups of all breeds and ages should be eating are raw meats and raw eggs, topped with a few fresh-cut vegetables. (The latter is for your satisfaction – dogs and cats don't care.)

However, this isn't common knowledge to pet owners because of a vast vegetarian conspiracy, conscious or subconscious. (Most of it is subconscious, in my opinion, but the end result is the same — bad health and an early death from what was formerly human diseases only.) As a result, a growing number of American — and now apparently some Canadian — pets are getting sick and dying of melamine poisoning, all but proven to be caused by tainted Chinese pet-food ingredients bought on-the-cheap by companies that care more for bottom lines than pets' lives. Do you think the Chinese care about the lives of our pets? – Look, in 2008 it was reported world wide that Chinese food manufactures illegally added melamine to baby food consumed in China!

In itself, this isn't so surprising, in my view. Capitalism can be cruel and corrupt, just like government. But capitalism combined with free enterprise is the only system that works in the long run. The trouble is, there isn't much free enterprise any more.

But now, there's evidence that this murderous conspiracy of greed isn't just threatening Felix and Fido. Melamine poisoning could soon land some of your friends (or even you) in the hospital or morgue if the worst-case scenario being reported comes to fruition.

According to the Associated Press and other sources, huge quantities of the more than 100 brands of tainted pet foods that have been pulled from store shelves since 2007 have found their way into hog-feed in as many as 6 U.S. states. Safety officials have quarantined hogs in California, New York, both Carolinas, Utah and Ohio. The urine of some of these quarantined hogs has tested positive for melamine poisoning, the FDA has reported.

It isn't known at this time whether any contaminated hogs have reached consumers' plates or not. Also implicated is at least one poultry farm, according to the FDA's chief veterinarian. Beyond this, the FDA has announced its intention to investigate other human foods that may have been subjected to contamination by these tainted Chinese grains — things like pizza dough, protein shakes, energy bars, and even infant formula.

There is a paradox about China. It is obvious that quality control in foods and medications is shabby at best. Remember the tragedy in Panama where many patients died from contaminated medicine shipped there from China via Europe?

The paradox is that China produces many high quality products, such as solar equipment, L.E.D. light products, vehicles, and just about everything you can imagine. My admonition is: don't eat anything produced in China and don't inject anything made there either.

## ENOUGH IS ENOUGH

The number of children sickened by chemical-tainted milk has reached almost 53,000 and countries from Asia to Africa have banned this product.

Products of 22 companies have been found selling melamine-contaminated dairy foods. A Bloomberg press release has announced that Taiwan has banned all dairy products from China. Nestle and Japanese

Marudai Foods have banned the products too. A note of interest: Arkansas-based Tyson Foods have in the past and present, "worked with" China's food regulator. Has "working with" the Chinese, by Tyson and others been effective? Contaminated sea food, tooth Paste, "nutrients," toys, and pet-killing foods – what next? Here's the outlook from Tyson's Jim Rice, "greater China country manager," in Arkansas: "That shows that they're serious, now this means a new guy with new ideas and maybe a new quality assurance system. It could be a healthy shakeup."

Maybe Tyson Foods needs a little shaking up for "working with" people who are irresponsible, crooked, and uncontrollable. The same can be said for Nestle, especially in Africa, but that's another sordid story. (See my book, The Raw Truth About Milk - www.drdouglass. com, for the Nestle report.)

(Bloomberg.com, September 22, 2008)

Time will tell whether this scandal becomes as deadly a risk to people as it has been to their pets. With the FDA doing the "oversight," we may never know the whole story. I think we are in dire need of more oversight of the oversighters. But perhaps the most infuriating aspect of this tragedy is that it's all based on a lie that's been systematically perpetrated by the vegetarian movement. In effect, they are the prime movers in this bloody mess.

At the beginning of this book, I pointed the finger of blame for this pet-food conspiracy — and all its casualties — squarely at— vegetarianism. In case you haven't put the big picture together, let me sum it up for you...

Not surprisingly, the pet food industry in this country has been infiltrated and taken over by a branch of the animal rights crowd. Not the most militant, mind you, but destructive enough. The worst of the lot believe that animal ownership by humans is as evil as animal slaughter for consumption. But these wackos are just a small percentage of the animal rights movement. It's the moderate bearhuggers, the vegetarians, which have caused the major damage to your dog's health.

A great many mainstream "animal people" are enthusiastic pet owners who believe in bonding with and loving animals. Unfortunately, a lot of them don't believe in eating animals or even allowing their animals to eat animals — even though it's exactly what their cats and dogs need to be healthy. A lot of them are vegetarians, and by default, their pets are too. But not all of them are. Plenty of dog and cat owners are meat-eaters, but they still want to buy what's best for their pets.

So they buy their pet-food on the advice of the "experts" at the local Petco or PetSmart, despite the fact that these stores are largely staffed by young, idealistic folks — many of whom buy into the vegetarian dogma hook, line and sinker. The whole thing combines to become a snowball effect.

Pet owners and buyers of all types get care and feeding advice from misguided people who are convinced that eating meat is cruelty to animals. This creates more demand for meatless pet-food — which spurs pet-food makers to buy ever-larger quantities of the cheapest vegetable ingredients that are still high in protein (even if they've been spiked with poisonous additives and it is the <u>wrong type of protein</u> for cats and dogs in the first place). Naturally, the cheapest of these are outside the U.S. And as such, they're low quality, un-regulated, and more likely to be hazardous.

Bottom line: If vegetarian dogma did not exist, pet owners, pet-store staffers, and veterinarians would wake up and take notice of what most animals eat naturally — each other. They'd also start allowing this knowledge to guide their dietary advice to pet owners, instead of allowing their own ignorance and prejudices to spur the death and sickening of countless numbers of the very pets for whom they purport to cherish and respect.

The reported number of 10,000 deaths for dogs and cats could be very much higher.

**Internet scams and pet food recalls: Who will cash in next? — the self-appointed experts with no training but a cool web site.**

With the tainted pet food debacle head-lining mainstream media earlier this year, I know you've been inundated with information regarding the quality of your pet's food. (In fact, plenty of that information came from the hand of yours truly.) But sit tight: This isn't just another treatise of mine warning you about what you're feeding your pets—instead, I'm warning you about what you're feeding <u>your mind</u> as well.

The Internet is fraught with outrageous, pseudo scientific claims that are harmful to the general welfare of its readers. The pet food scandal happens to be a perfect example of that.

Overnight, dozens of "kibble experts" crawled out of the woodwork, all claiming that their pet food was the safest, most nutritious source available. Fat chance. If these gold-diggers weren't telling you to feed your pets a completely raw food diet, then the only thing their information should feed is the woodstove. Naturopath Lisa Newman is no different than the rest of them.

If you want to drive yourself crazy, read Lisa's report on commercial dog food. Her opus, which is tens of pages long, says that all commercial dog food (or certainly most of it) is made from the cheapest ingredients available. She and her associates examined <u>448 pet food products</u> and then conducted a nutritional analysis of each ingredient in each product—a monumental achievement, and an even more monumental waste of time.

In none of the Newman material I read (and it took considerable time to read it all) is there any mention of <u>the root cause</u> of why commercial dog food is toxic to your pet. There's no denying that commercial dog food is comprised of nutritionally deficient ingredients, pesticides, dies, and preservatives. But in the end, they're toxic to your pet simply because they're <u>cooked</u>.

I wanted to give Lisa the benefit of the doubt. So just to make sure I wasn't somehow missing a new and great feeding break-through, I investigated her website.

## A sucker is born every day

What I found on Lisa's website should come as no surprise: She's selling her own brand of dog food. As it turns out, Lisa wasn't on a mission to expose the commercial pet food industry—she was on a mission to market her own products.

She points an accusing finger at most commercial pet foods, saying they contain waste products, inferior ingredients, incorrect ingredients, and "gimmicks"—all the while claiming that <u>her</u> products are of the highest quality. I have no doubt that her claims about her competitors are true. But is the pot calling the kettle black? Does your dog need "Flower Essences for Emotions"? Does your dog need menadione sodium bisulfate complex as a vitamin K supplement?

Nowhere on her site could I find sources of FRESH, RAW animal fat and animal protein, such as raw chicken, raw hamburger, raw chicken liver, raw milk, and, especially, RAW BONES—the very essence of the ideal diet for your dog.

## Self-proclaimed expert creates an alternate reality

Finally, I found out why. After hours of digging around through all the pseudo-science, I came to the truth about Lisa Newman: <u>She is opposed to the natural diet of raw foods upon which dogs thrive</u>. Her reasoning:

"It is shown that a long term B.A.R.F. (biologically appropriate raw food) diet is likely to decrease the overall health of the pet. The pet's ability to digest the raw foods is compromised by evolutionary changes to the digestive tracts of domesticated pets. The difficulty in digesting raw foods combined with this evolutionary weakness creates a systematic breakdown of immune responses, leading to a variety of nutritionally-based symptoms."

And what is her documentation for throwing out the natural food of your pet? Her own article, of course, which was not published in any accredited scientific journal—or even an unaccredited one, as far as I can determine. The whole thing (with the proper "evolutionary," politically correct jargon thrown in) is a blatant promotion of her superior "beyond natural" supplements and canned cooked food.

## I think, therefore I am a ...

Now, let me assure you that <u>I am not an elitist</u>. My great grandmother, Lucy Bell, was the only doctor in Cherokee Country, Georgia, after the Yankees burned everything to the ground. She was greatly respected and a legend in her time. She was an herbalist.

On the matter of licensing professionals in any trade—including the practice of medicine—I would consider myself a "libertarian anarchist." To state it hyperbolically, if you want to see a podiatrist for the treatment of your brain tumor, then that's your right. Licensing by the government—local, state, or federal—is counterproductive in the long run. It leads to corruption and monopoly. Liberty, freedom of action by individuals, are always better.

The caveat to that: <u>you must think for yourself</u>. If you don't, the government has no problem doing it for you. Most organizations have rules and standards to which its members are expected to comply. (This is obviously not true of the junk pet food industry.) With something as serious as your health and your pet's health, you need to check out the group to which you are entrusting your life.

If you have a urological problem (and if you have any common sense), you should see a naturopath first (except for emergencies). If he can't help you, then see if an urologist can help solve your problem. No matter what course of action you take, there is no guarantee. Still, at the end of your search, you must think for yourself — and for your pet.

## PET HOLOCAUST

This exposé is going to be jaw-dropper. It is so astounding that we must be absolutely sure of the facts. The vets seem strangely silent on this horrific scandal and tragedy. That is because many of them are involved in the commercial pet food racket and peddle kibble from their offices.

The story going around is that pets taken to a vet for euthanasia are delivered to rendering plants and then sold to pet food companies to be used as pet food.

I'm not sure I believe this but do you remember Mad Cow disease? I didn't believe that at first either. Would the Brits, animal-lovers all, allow their cows to be fed the carcasses of sheep or any animal for that matter? They didn't "allow" it but it happened in secret. Mad Cow is a neurological disease caused by the ingestion of central nervous system tissue (brains primarily) by cows from

slaughtered sheep in commercial "beef opera-
tions. In the sheep the disease" is called "scra-
pie." In a cow it is called Mad Cow because
the cow literally goes mad. A related variant
in humans is called Krutzfeld-Jacob disease.
It causes brain rot and a fairly quick death.
One more relative is known as Kuru. It came
from New Guinea where certain tribes used
to eat other tribes, especially their brains, to
smarten themselves up a bit.

Kuru was "introduced" to the U.S. by a
repulsive character, Dr Carleton Gaduchek,
who worked in the biological warfare depart-
ment of the U.S. Army, Fort Detrick, Maryland. He had a Chinese Communist wife, was
an avid admirer of Lenin, and he had a full
size-picture of Lenin in his office. (No, I am
not making this up.) Gaduchek had glass jars
of Kuru-infected human brains shipped to
him at Ft. Detrick from New Guinea. Carleton
Gaduchek was a brilliant man and received a
Nobel Prize for his work on the discovery of
prions, a micro-organism smaller than a virus
which is what all these neurological maladies
apparently are.

With a character like Gaduchek <u>right in
the center of the AIDS epidemic</u>, at the place
where it is presumed to have been created

– Ft. Detrick, Maryland – makes one wonder if AIDS is related to these awful diseases.

I'm not quite as far off the subject as you might imagine. A group of enraged and heart-broken pet owners, mostly untrained in biological science, have been asking around and have found a few vets willing to speak out on this deplorable scandal – but only confidentially. If we confirm what we have been reading, the pet food companies and the vets are in serious trouble.

Andrew Lewis was one of the first to expose this news, below is a letter I sent to him (no reply so far!):

LETTER TO A CONCERNED PET LOVER
Mr. Andrew Lewis
MIAMI FLORIDA
USA

**Dear Mr. Lewis:**

I have read your material on the pet holocaust with great interest. I have been railing against the commercial pet food racket for a number of years and, understanding the extent of the racket, I agree with you in almost every respect. Being very familiar with the mad cow story, I can believe just about anything concerning the feeding of pets with commercial pet food, including the use of cat and dog carcasses recycled for pet food.

From a cold-blooded scientific point of view, there is nothing wrong with it since dogs and cats are carnivores designed by their Maker to eat other animals, including humans, dogs and cats if found rotting in a field. They are all carnivores and cannibals when it is necessary to survive. This is true of humans as well. In World War II, in Leningrad when Hitler's troops besieged the city for 900 days, the people were starving and cannibalism was a thriving business. It was strictly forbidden, punishable by death to sell human flesh, but the meat lockers were available to those who knew. The Nomenclatura and the military, naturally, got the best cuts. There were no dogs and cats on the streets and few in the apartments as they had been eaten long before.

However, this is unacceptable in our society where we have anthropomorphized our pets. We are "wealthy" and the idea of starvation is simply not in our experience except in the history books. When I was in the sixth grade I remember our teacher telling us about the "starving Armenians." In college I learned about the "starving Ukrainians." I didn't know where Armenia was and I had never heard of the Ukraine. But it didn't matter because those things didn't happen in our secure world. I have digressed a bit but my point is, to repeat, there is nothing wrong about recycling animals for food for carnivorous animals.

Doing so for ruminants, i.e. vegetarian animals, is'going against nature and was bound to cause trouble. Mad Cow Disease was the result.

If you can verify for me that the practice of recycling pets for pet food is indeed extant, I would appreciate the documentation. My investigators attempted to contact two veterinarians mentioned in your report. One never responded and the other was "in a hurry" and non-committal.

*If this recycling is going on, I don't think it will be stopped. If you have a beloved pet, as most of us do, and you can't stand the idea of it becoming dog or cat food, there are three ways to salve your conscience: (1) Take the suffering animal into your back yard, shoot it in the head and bury it there. I have a friend who, being a tough guy, did just that. He loved his dog deeply. Most pet owners in the Western World couldn't do it. I think he made the right decision. (2) Take your friend to a vet, have him "put to sleep" and insist that he be immediately cremated and you take the ashes home. (3) Take your loved one to a vet to be euthanized, tell him not to sell the body but dispose of it in a decent manner — and walk away.*

This letter started out as a simple inquiry as to the veracity of the claim that pets are being recycled into pet food. I hope you will excuse my excursions into related matters and I look forward to your reply.

A "PS" to the above letter: On investigating the above web site, I discovered the writer of this expose' is himself promoting his own miracle dog chow <u>comprised of cooked food</u>. Even people who mean well and fret for their pets are urging the worst possible diets.

Here's a letter written to me which I will use to expose yet another miscreant in this massive dog food scam. (I promise this will be the last of my traducements of this unspeakable and virulently poisonous industry.)

Dear Dr Douglass:

"There's a really convincing ad on the internet for a dog food product from Hill's. It's called the *Science Diet* and has the *Nature's Best* label but its <u>Hill's Pet Nutrition, Inc</u>. They claim their new *Science Diet* is 'the first and only natural pet food clinically proven to provide complete, balanced nutrition.' This statement is attributed to one Kim Friesen, Ph.D., who is the "pet nutritionist" for Hill's Pet Nutrition, Inc. I think I know what your reply will be but perhaps some of your readers haven't read your excellent expose' on the subject of commercial pet food and would benefit from your opinion. After all, they're claiming: 'Helping all pets live naturally' ". — J.R., NM

Thanks, J.R., for the "heads-up" on the latest pet nutrition scam.

I would like Dr Friesen to explain to us what "complete, balanced nutrition" is and how their wonder food was "clinically proven" to deserve these accolades. The "Science Diet" is simply another kibble product with some added bad features. First, as you know <u>kibble equals cooked</u> and that means the product fails at the starter gate. Your dog should not eat ANY cooked food — PERIOD. The "Science Diet" contains soy derivatives which are not fit for animal or human consumption. Please read my article on soy in the ... Issue of the Douglass Letter. They may get "real chicken" from a commercial chicken prison but when it arrives at your dog's food pan it is bone-free (and so relatively nutrition-free), tasteless, and it doesn't look like chicken; it looks like what it is — KIBBLE — a largely vegetarian non-food not fit for a possum or even a Petco executive.

This product will lead your dog to the same fate as most American dogs — diabetes, heart disease, kidney failure, arthritis and an early death. The animal will look great for the first four to five years (youth can cover a lot of nutrition sins) and after that deterioration is often rapid. The vet will suggest a "special medical formula" at three times the price — but it will still be KIBBLE and the dog will die.

**Visit www.hillspet.com for a listing of ingredients of the 'Science Diet' product clearly list Soy derivatives.**

# SUMMARY

Well, that's it. I've tricked you into reading all the above because if I hadn't, you wouldn't have believed these simple admonitions on how to feed your pet. And if you care about petdom as much as you do Christendom (or almost as much), ask your friends to *buy this book*. If they don't buy the book, (1) they won't believe the simple summary below and (2) *I won't make any money.*

Foods your dog should *not* eat:

- Sugar and Sugar substitutes (Aspartame will kill your dog — and you.)
- Raisins
- Onions
- Chocolate
- Starch, such as bread and potatoes
- Pasteurized, homogenized, condensed, soy, powdered, chocolate or skimmed milk
- Cooked food of *any kind* which means...
- Commercial (or even fresh) fruit juices. The only three fruits our two perfect dogs like are tomatoes, avocado, and bananas (sometimes). Their favorite, paws down, is avocado. They will often

eat it before their beloved hamburger. If your dog is prone to obesity, leave out the banana. They will often eat raw fruit, such as mango and papaya, found on the grounds of our property *if it is rotten or, at least, very ripe.*

- Coke, Pepsi, and other carbonated drinks
- Alcoholic beverages
- Fluoridated, chlorinated water. It amazes me how many dog owners who truly want the best for their pets will feed them tap water, which usually contains both of the above, while they personally drink bottled water.
- *TOFU*: "Toe Fou No Goo Fo U" — or your dog.

It may be the nutritional phylactery of the vegetarian crowd but, believe me, *tofu is a killer.* I don't understand how people can eat this stuff. The only thing good I can say about it is: its tender. Jell-O is tender as well but do you think of it as *actual food*? (Hospital dieticians seem to think so.)

Lon R. White, MD, with the Pacific Health Institute in Honolulu, Hawaii, has made some stunning discoveries concerning the deleterious effects of tofu on the brain. This is not just one of those weirdo hoaxes found on the internet. This is the real thing.

You can read it yourself:

- *Tragedy and Hype,"* Third International Soy Symposium, **Nexus,** April/May 2000

- *Neurobiological Aging,* 1996, 7, suppl 4 S121; **Journal of the American Medical Assoc.,** 1996 276, 955-960

- *Brain Aging and Midlife Tofu Consumption,"* **Journal of the American College of Nutrition,** 2000, 19, 207-209 and 242-255

- *The Whole Soy Story,* http://www. newtrendspublishing.com/

The later source will really inform you about the whole soy disaster.

Tofu is made from soy beans *and most commercial dog foods contain soy derivatives.* Here is what Doctors White and Petrovitch discovered:

If you eat two or more servings of tofu per week during midlife (I guess that means age 5 to 7 for your dog.), you are more likely to suffer **brain atrophy** and **dementia** later in life than those who haven't partaken of this "health food."

Magnetic resonance imaging and autopsies confirmed their clinical impressions gained from psychological testing. "Alzheimer's disease", decrease in thinking ability ("cognitive decline"), and dementia were more common among tofu eaters. The ventricles (cavities) of the brain were found to be enlarged and the brains were shrunken and low in weight.

Our technology has become so advanced that we can now use humans for detecting certain diseases rather than experimental animals. Now we need to do a similar study on BARF-fed ("**B**iologically **A**ppropriate **R**aw **F**oods") dogs compared to vegetarian fed (i.e. all commercial dog foods) dogs. We know what the answers will be and it will revolutionize dogdem — and catdem. This is the only way we can convince the American people — and the rest of the modern world — that the commercial pet food industry is the reason for the dramatic increase among pets of cancer, arthritis, diabetes, hypertension, heart disease, and renal disease. All of these conditions were rare among dogs and cats before the mid-20th Century.

I'll add an important codicil to this indictment of soy: Fermented soy foods are OK to eat but your dog will not be interested.

- Commercially prepared "treats" and...
- *NO KIBBLE OR OTHER COMMER-CIAL PET FOOD*

## WHAT YOUR DOG AND CAT SHOULD EAT:

- Raw milk – unlimited quantities
- Raw eggs – unlimited quantities
- Boneless fish (Actually, they can eat raw fish with bones but I'm squeamish about it, the dogs aren't)
- Any mammalian or avian fat, muscle and offal

With this simple diet, they need no vitamin, mineral, or herbal supplements.

Let me back off on this advice a little bit.

My great-grandmother, Lucy Bell, who lived to the age of 99, was an herbalist, now known as a naturopath, and was the only doctor/surgeon in Cherokee County, Georgia, after General Sherman burned everything to the ground, leaving the populace (what was left of it) sick and dying. Believe me; the people loved my Grandma Lucy. See note on page 45.

I brought up the Grandma Bell story on page 45 for two reasons: (1) I like to tell it and (2) For her advice on cod liver oil:

"Billy, if you take cod liver oil every day, you ain't ever gonna to be sick." I believed her but didn't take her advice because it was so repulsive. Once it was encapsulated, about twenty years ago, I started taking it twice daily and have never missed a day.

My dogs don't get any fish, not even rotten fish — which I am sure they would like — but they get one capsule of cod liver oil daily in their food pan. They don't just swallow it as I do; they *chew* it — they love it! Don't try this on your kibble dog until he has been converted to the BARF diet.

## GARLIC NEEDS SPECIAL MENTION

Garlic has had a tough time of it. In spite of hundreds of years of preserving and improving the health of untold millions of humans, modern chemical identification and analysis of plant forms put a tinge of doubt in the minds of some moderns, including scientists, about the safety of garlic in animal feeding.

There's no doubt that onions are toxic to dogs and cats and they are similar chemically. Onion is Allium cepa and garlic is Allium sativum. They are both flavorful; they have the same color, more or less; and they are both HOT in the mouth. In fact, garlic looks like "spring onions" ("scallions") when it is growing. But just because they have the same family name (Allium) doesn't mean they are the same. The onion is from the cepa branch of the family. It's OK for humans (especially on medium rare hamburger) but *deadly* for dogs. (Trust me on this; I'm a wannabe veterinarian.) The confusion has come from the thiosulfate content in onion — toxic for sure in dogs — but only present in minute amounts in cousin Allium sativum (garlic).

The thiosulfate content of the Allium family requires a little clarification. Heinz Factor Anemia is a "hemolytic" condition where the red blood cells "lyse" or break open leading to severe anemia and often death of the dog. Garlic and onion both contain thiosulfate but the amount in garlic is minute and unimportant. But there is enough in onion to make it deadly to dogs. The misconception about garlic is so widespread that there has been a near panic on the subject. Even one animal poison control center has entered a warning of the dangers of garlic in dogs! There are other agents that cause this anemia, Tylenol and benzocaine topical anesthesia, for example. But onion is the major culprit.

Truly, garlic should be called "Vitamin G" when it comes to dog nutrition. It will give your dog <u>a luminous coat</u> (It won't hurt yours either). It is excellent for warding off intestinal parasites, <u>eliminating the need for the periodic worming that most vets advocate</u>. Garlic protects your pet from ticks and fleas. It is claimed (but not proven) that garlic prevents cancer, diabetes, heart ailments and just about every other human disease.

For social reasons, we don't give our perfect dogs garlic on the weekends. We have our social functions on the weekends — Friday, Saturday, or Sunday. Garlic gives your dog garlic breath and garlic B.O. — just as it does to you. We love to show off our radiantly healthy "children" so we give them high-octane raw hamburger (chopped fresh garlic mixed in) only on Mondays, Tuesdays, or Wednesdays.

Parenthetically, Hannibal and Silky have the sweetest breath in the world, better than mine I guarantee you. A kibble dog has terrible breath and rotten teeth which makes the halitosis worse. And while I'm being parenthetical, their stools are minimally odiferous, and small in amount. This is because *they are not overloaded with fiber* as factory-fed dogs are. I think fiber is overrated for both dogs and humans but the junk food industry sells *a lot* of breakfast cereal - "The Breakfast of Champions," as Michael Jordan will assure you - by promoting a "high-fiber diet." All it does is give you bigger stools — and less room in your diet for real food.

In ancient Europe there was a strong belief that garlic warded off werewolves, demons and vampires. Try it and report back to me.

## THE CONVERSION TO BARF — NOT ALWAYS EASY

Here's a letter that illustrates a common problem when you convert your dog to his natural diet:

> "I took your advice and fed my dog raw liver, raw chicken necks, and raw eggs. He lost weight and looked really sick. What happened? – T.K., FL

Any mammal will often get sick when his diet is suddenly changed, even when you are changing to a <u>better</u> diet. It works the same in humans. When vegetarians see the light and start eating meat, they are often disappointed at first because of this phenomenon. Put your dog back on the dang kibble but give him a raw egg, including the shell, with it. This will be a great step forward and, in fact, will make up for many of the deficiencies of the vegetarian diet he has been eating. Over a period of about a month, add gradually chicken necks to the kibble with the skin on them. (Hard to find because the butcher thinks he is doing you a favor by removing the skin – cardiologists, playing nutritionist, have (mal) advised heart patients to remove the skin from their chicken in order to avoid "all that nasty cholesterol and fat," thus losing about half of the nutritional value.) Then start adding the chicken liver as you decrease the kibble. We used to give them kibble only as filler on top as we thought they liked the crunch. But we decided the crunch wasn't worth the risk — carrots and chicken necks give them all the "crunch" they need. And don't forget the raw pork, lamb or beef joint daily in the morning. Raw chicken bones are also excellent — no, they will not splinter if they are <u>fresh</u>.

Cats can (and should) eat a diet that is 100 percent liver, CHICKEN LIVER. They really don't need anything else. (Cats are more adaptable than dogs. They can eat just about anything and survive to an old age.) With dogs, restrict the chicken liver to about 25 percent of the portion but definitely give it daily or at least three times a week. (A standard measuring cup full is sufficient.) I may have forgotten to mention that raw hamburger comprises about 25 percent of their diet and is given daily. We seldom leave out the chicken necks and NEVER leave out the raw egg. Buy the cheapest priced hamburger because, ironically, it is the most nutritious; it contains the most fat. YOU should eat it too. (Medium rare)

One of our dogs, a Weimaraner, has eaten this diet since six weeks of age. She is now four years-old and is all bone and muscle, covered with the most beautiful coat I have ever seen – 70 pounds of boundless energy.

## Buying and storing your pet's fresh cuisine

Modern refrigeration has revolutionized food storage.

Buy the cheapest grade of hamburger with maximum marbling (fat) for maximum nutrition.

Buy five or ten pounds at a time. If you have had the hamburger in the fridge unfrozen for a few days, it might turn a little green. But don't worry about it; your friend is color blind and, anyway, he *likes* his food on the ripe side. In the Arctic, in the early 20th Century, the natives ate frozen, rotten fish. It was considered a delicacy. (Never eat rotten fish in the summer; it will make you sick.)

Purchase chicken necks *with the skin intact* (most of the fat is just under the skin). Most doctors advise their patients to eat chicken without the skin. This removes 50 percent of the food value. If your dog or cat eats chicken with the skin intact, he'll be healthier than you. Buy five or ten pounds at a time and freeze it.

Chicken livers are very important, *especially for your cat*. Felix and Fanny can live a perfectly healthy and happy life *eating nothing but raw chicken livers*. My two sibling cats, Pistol and Paint, have eaten nothing but raw chicken livers their entire lives. (When you buy it from a butcher, the heart is also included. In New Guinea, they say eating hearts from animals — or humans — gives you courage.) Pistol and paint are 15 years old and enjoying perfect health.

A caveat: inspect the liver for presence of the gall bladder. It's a pea-size, brilliant green sack, easy to see. It tastes terrible even to a dog or cat so cut it out without cutting into it.

Some dogs don't like chicken liver and calf liver even less. That's unfortunate but keep trying; it's worth the effort. If all else fails, put it in your blender and blend enough to break it up into small pieces. Mix a little into the hamburger.

Our Basset, Hannibal Douglass, is a gourmand type of eater. You put his pan on the floor; he looks at it; he looks at you; then, if you encourage him, he may start eating. He would always smell the liver and then toss it on the floor with a flick of his cute little snout. After he finished all the good stuff — the necks, the hamburger, the avocado — the carrot pieces, the green pepper, and the tomato slices were leisurely munched on. (He's the only dog I know that eats slower than I do.) Then, and only then, would he amble over to the liver, look back at me ("Do I *have* to eat this?") and chew on the slimy stuff. He rarely finished it.

And then I made an important serendipitous discovery that negates all that trickery concerning liver mentioned above.

One evening when Hannibal was about two years old, I had to feed him the liver frozen. We were running late for a dinner engagement so I just tossed it on the top his sumptuous raw dinner. He put it between his incisors and, as usual, dropped it on the floor. He studied it, smelled it and then started eating it with the greatest of pleasure. He didn't touch any of his gourmet dinner until the liver was devoured. Eureka! — a perfect popsicle for dogs. (I call it a liver-sicle.) Incidentally, I was surprised to discover that they don't mind eating <u>everything</u> frozen — necks, hamburger and all.

You can use the same trickery on your cat if necessary. ***Raw chicken liver is essential for your cat*** and they tend to love it.

All of these foods can be kept frozen for months without losing much food value but we buy their victuals fresh about once a week.

All mammalian and avian meat is good for your pet: lamb, pork, beef, chicken, duck, goose, armadillo, rats, mice, rabbits (especially rabbit liver) — and the bones from all these creatures.

For a medium size dog, 30 to 50 pounds, use the medium size "zip-lock" plastic bags (8 by 7 inches), one for each serving. Put into the bag two chicken livers and the rest divided between the necks and the hamburger. Even better, freeze the chicken liver separately.

Then you can unfreeze the hamburger/chicken necks and place the frozen liver on top of their food. They will eat the "liversicle" first.

You can add the fruits and veggies if you like. Your pet doesn't care. He doesn't need variety (They are creatures of habit.) and they do not need fruits and vegetables at all. These additions are for *your* satisfaction as it makes you think your pal is getting a "more balanced diet." Well, OK, but please don't overdo it.

Again, I must temper my remarks on fruits and vegetables in the above paragraph. Some vets with years of experience do feel that your pet needs some fruits and vegetables. They point out that the first thing they go for on making a kill is the rumen in the stomach. The rumen is the first part of the stomach in plant-eating animals. It is where the plant cellulose is broken down so that the vegetable matter can be properly digested. Your dog does not have that ability so feeding him plants with cellulose around the food particles is a waste of time if it is raw. Parenthetically, you can derive nourishment from high-fiber foods, such as carrots, because you chew your food (I hope); your dog essentially swallows it whole. He may bite into a piece of carrot the size of a crap-game dice but then down it goes.

I know this sounds a bit contradictory, but you must "par-boil" hard vegetables, such as carrots, or they are not digestible to your dog — or to you — if you eat like a dog. A good alternative, if you are determined to "vegetarianize" your dog, is to run all high-fiber fruits and vegetables through a blender. As I have iterated above, they like very ripe or rotten fruits and vegetables. That's because the God of the Dogs, Caninus Magnus, has broken down the cellulose (fiber) and thus has made it digestible.

We feed our pet-children about six PM daily. (Remember, they like an ordered life.) They get a special treat first thing in the morning – a nice raw beef or pork joint bone. Then they have a few slurps of Daddy's famous cold-brewed coffee-with-cream poured on the floor. Then they get a generous splash of raw milk on the floor. They will drink it as long as I pour it, putting to rest the old story that "no animal but Man drinks milk after weaning." This is generally true because *they don't have access to it*.

Caveat: Don't feed them pasteurized milk; better no milk at all — it's *cooked* and not good for dogs or humans.

For our medium size pets we like the bones about half the size of a man's fist. If they are young, it might take them hours to eat it but they don't mind.

Flat bones are not desirable as they tend to get lodged in the hard palate of the mouth. This is terrifying to the owner but really not hard to cure. Just stick your finger in his mouth, get under the bone and dislodge it. He's not going to choke and he's not going to bite you. Also, the flat bones tend to be extremely hard to break. They may abandon such a bone after eating off the meat and fat. If I see them on the floor unattended, I toss them in the waste basket.

## FIBER

Fiber has enjoyed the status of an essential nutrient in the past 30 years. It has even been claimed that it will prevent diabetes and heart disease. I don't think this has been proven. While I haven't investigated it, I feel certain that the grain, bean and cereal industries financed this misconception through grants to various university nutrition departments.

Our dogs have small stools because they get very little fiber. (Remember: the smaller the stool, the smaller the time spent in animal hospital.) The same applies to humans — fiber is overrated.

# A FEW QUIBBLES WITH DR. BILLINGHURST

I have a few quibbles with Dr. Billing-hurst but they're only quibbles and are in no way meant to denigrate his work. If you are only interested in the diet and not philosophy, skip the next four paragraphs. (But record the Web site at the bottom.)

Dr. Billinghurst refers on many pages to the "evolution" of the dog and his eating habits. I doubt that the dog's dietary preferences have changed in the last 100 years or even in the last 1000 years. There is *genetic variation* between breeds but that is not evolution. Evolution is the crack-brained theory of one Charles Darwin who hypothesized that lower species "evolve" upward to superior species by "survival of the fittest." It is obvious that the smart and the strong in the wilds of nature are more likely to survive than the weak and the stupid. That is *genetic variation* and has nothing to do with evolution, the changing of one species into another.

After one hundred years of dedicated search, *not one missing link* has been found that would prove evolution caused mice, for instance, to develop wings because of the "evolutionary advantage" of flying and thus became bats. Dr Billinghurst's work is not *evolutionary* but it is certainly ***revolutionary***. It is revolutionary because it completely refutes the modern belief that your dog should be a vegetarian. (He <u>does</u> think dogs (but not cats) benefit from eating fruits and vegetables. I don't think they benefit enough to make it necessary.)

My only other quibble is that I think he is too kind to the vegetarians who make their dogs eat a vegetarian diet. I don't think these misinformed and fanatic vegans should be given any slack at all. I would tell them (And do tell them): "Making your dog into a vegan is preposterous nonsense. He, like you, is an omnivore and more carnivore than herbivore. Wake up and smell the sausages. If you want to go to an early grave for your veganism, that's up to you — but it's not fair to take your dog with you."

It is true that your pet will, if it gets the opportunity, take its own kill in the wild and eat everything but the fur. Oh what a thrill that must be! He'll probably lay it on the front doorstep in order to receive your well-deserved approbation: "Look: Daddy, I caught this rabbit on the run — is that great or what?"

# THE ONE OTHER DOG DIET BOOK YOU NEED TO READ

## — *Give Your Dog a Bone* — by Ian Billinghurst, DVM

I recommend that you purchase it directly from the author in Australia. The American distributor seems to be more interested in selling their version of the BARF (Biologically-Appropriate Raw Food) diet through distributorships on the internet rather than in selling the book. In order to purchase the book, I was required to join up, which I declined. Whatever they are selling, you can purchase from your local butcher — fresh and RAW.

The web site is:
www.barfaustralia.com.au.

If you read <u>this</u> book and Dr Billinghurst's book, *GIVE YOUR DOG A BONE*, you will double the lifespan of your pet. If you buy <u>his</u> book, then you will not need to purchase <u>my</u> book. But I suppose you have already done that — SORRY.

A final word: SAY NO TO PETCO — <u>smell the bone and the liver</u> and give your pet-child a chance for a long, healthy, and loving life with you and the rest of your family.

# What about cats?

# What about cats?

I don't want to be accused of ignoring cats in this book. Well it's true. I did ignore them because I have always considered cats to be tougher and more adaptable than dogs — none of that loyalty and lovey-dovie stuff — except on their terms. I still think it is true in a general sense but I was wrong on a number of parameters. If you have an in-and-out cat, he will make up for your kibble transgressions by eating mice, birds, lizards (overindulgence in this delicacy will make them sick — they quickly learn), snakes and an occasional rabbit.

But if you have a completely indoor cat, and you feed him nothing but cooked food — and, remember, all commercial animal food is cooked — then he is headed for an early dog heaven (which would be a cat hell). I was reminded of this by reading a seminal little book, _Pottenger's Cats_, by Francis M. Pottenger, Jr., MD. The research was done over 50 years ago and presaged the current tragedy we are seeing in all pets because of not getting a raw animal food diet.

Pottenger came about his remarkable discovery by accident. Pottenger was experimenting in the production of adrenal cortical extract (ACE). This extract of the adrenal extract is very effective in the treatment of many diseases. But there was no effective way at the time to measure the potency of the extracts. Dr. Pottenger used stray cats to determine the potency of the ACE samples. He would operate on the cat, remove their adrenal glands and then determine how much of the ACE would keep the animal alive. That would determine its potency. This is crude by current laboratory science but that's all he had at the time.

Now here is where the serendipidity came in to play which led to Dr. Pottenger becoming a sage on animal health. Today he is almost forgotten — except among the raw-food cognizant (like you and me). Pottenger was puzzled as to why his cats had a low resistance to his surgery. He was using the best techniques of the day but many of the cats seemed to die early after surgeries in what looked like a nutritional deficiency. Those who survived and had kittens had deformed babies. He was feeding his cats cooked scraps donated by neighbors. As the number of cats donated by neighbors increased, the amount of donated scraps remained the same, resulting in a food shortage for his animals. So he contracted with a local meat-packing plant to supply raw meat scraps, including the viscera as well as the meat. For reasons not explained (perhaps even to himself), he gave the raw food diet only to the new cats. The results were impressive. The raw-fed cats were in obvious good health, their offspring were vigorous and the operative mortality lessened dramatically.

Dr. Pottenger decided that this deserved a separate investigation and hence the Pottenger Cat Study began under the watchful eye of some of the most prominent pathologists of the day from the University of Southern California. The results were conclusive: raw animal food produced vibrantly healthy cats and cooked food led to death and disease. <u>These successful experiments have never been repeated and the whole project has been ignored</u> by "organized science."

You should read this book if you have a cat; you should read it even if you <u>don't</u> have a cat. If you don't have a cat, then you have a dog, husband, or some other animal to which you are attached. The book is available from: www.ppnf.org and info@ppnf.org.

The best food for cats:

Raw liver (chicken or rabbit) — The most essential food for cats. They can live well on nothing but fresh liver.

Raw milk

Raw chicken or any other type of bird — especially if they catch it and eat it immediately.

That's all there is to it.

You want to protect those you love from the health dangers the authorities aren't telling you about, and learn the incredible cures that they've scorned and ignored?
Subscribe to the free Daily Dose updates "...the straight scoop about health, medicine, and politics." by sending an e-mail to real_sub@agoramail.net with the word "subscribe" in the subject line.

**If you knew of a procedure that could save thousands, maybe millions, of people dying from AIDS, cancer, and other dreaded killers....**

# Would you cover it up?

It's unthinkable that what could be the best solution ever to stopping the world's killer diseases is being ignored, scorned, and rejected. But that is exactly what's happening right now.

The procedure is called "photoluminescence". It's a thoroughly tested, proven therapy that uses the healing power of the light to perform almost miraculous cures.

This remarkable treatment works its incredible cures by stimulating the body's own immune responses. That's why it cures so many ailments--and why it's been especially effective against AIDS! Yet, 50 years ago, it virtually disappeared from the halls of medicine.

Why has this incredible cure been ignored by the medical authorities of this country? You'll find the shocking answer here in the pages of this new edition of Into the Light. Now available with the blood irradiation Instrument Diagram and a complete set of instructions for building your own "Treatment Device". Also includes details on how to use this unique medical instrument.

*Into the Light*

*Into the Light*

Rhino Publishing S.A.
www.rhinopublish.com

### Dr. Douglass' Complete Guide to Better Vision

A report about eyesight and what can be done to improve it naturally. But I've also included information about how the eye works, brief descriptions of various common eye conditions, traditional remedies to eye problems, and a few simple suggestions that may help you maintain your eyesight for years to come.
-William Campbell Douglass II, MD

### The Hypertension Report.
### Say Good Bye to High Blood Pressure.

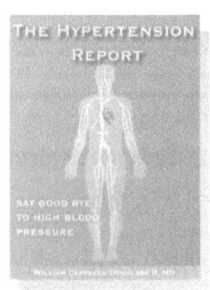

An estimated 50 million Americans have high blood pressure. Often called the "silent killer" because it may not cause symptoms until the patient has suffered serious damage to the arterial system. Diet, exercise, potassium supplements chelation therapy and practically anything but drugs is the way to go and alternatives are discussed in this report.

### Grandma Bell's A To Z Guide To Healing With Herbs.

This book is all about - coming home. What I once believed to be old wives' tales - stories long destroyed by the new world of science - actually proved to be the best treatment for many of the common ailments you and I suffer through. So I put a few of them together in this book with the sincere hope that Grandma Bell's wisdom will help you recover your common sense, and take responsibility for your own health.
-William Campbell Douglass II, MD

### Prostate Problems:
### Safe, Simple, Effective Relief for Men over 50.

Don't be frightened into surgery or drugs you may not need. First, get the facts about prostate problems... know all your options, so you can make the best decisions. This fully documented report explains the dangers of conventional treatments, and gives you alternatives that could save you more than just money!

**Rhino Publishing, S.A.**
**www.rhinopublish.com**

# Color me Healthy
## The Healing Powers
## of Colors

"He's crazy!"
"He's got to be a quack!"
"Who gave this guy his medical license?"
"He's a nut case!"

In case you're wondering, those are the reactions you'll probably get if
you show your doctor this report. I know the idea of healing many
common ailments simply by exposing them to colored light sounds far-
fetched, but when you see the evidence, you'll agree that color is truly
an amazing medical breakthrough.

When I first heard the stories,
I reacted much the same way.
But the evidence so
convinced me, that I had to
try color therapy in my practice.
My results were truly amazing.

**-William Campbell Douglass II, MD**

Order your complete set of Roscolene filters (choice of 3
sizes) to be used with the "Color Me Healthy" therapy. The
eleven Roscolene filters are # 809, 810, 818, 826, 828, 832,
859, 861, 866, 871, and 877. The filters come with protective
separator sheets between each filter. The color names and
the Roscolene filter(s) used to produce that particular color,
are printed on a card included with the filters
and a set of instructions on how to fit them to
a lamp.

**Rhino Publishing**
**www.rhinopublish.com**

# What Is Going on Here?

*Peroxides are supposed to be bad for you. Free radicals and all that. But now we hear that hydrogen peroxide is good for us. Hydrogen peroxide will put extra oxygen in your blood. There's no doubt about that. Hydrogen peroxide costs pennies. So if you can get oxygen into the blood cheaply and safely, maybe cancer (which doesn't like oxygen), emphysema, AIDS, and many other terrible diseases can be treated effectively. Intravenous hydrogen peroxide rapidly relieves allergic reactions, influenza symptoms, and acute viral infections.*

*No one expects to live forever. But we would all like to have a George Burns finish. The prospect of finishing life in a nursing home after abandoning your tricycle in the mobile home park is not appealing. Then comes the loss of control of vital functions the ultimate humiliation. Is life supposed to be from tricycle to tricycle and diaper to diaper? You come into this world crying, but do you have to leave crying? I don't believe you do. And you won't either after you see the evidence. Sounds too good to be true, doesn't it? Read on and decide for yourself.*

-William Campbell Douglass II, MD

Rhino Publishing S.A.
www.rhinopublish.com

HYDROGEN PEROXIDE

Medical Miracle

$H_2O$

# Eat Your Cholesterol!

### Eat Meat, Drink Milk, Spread The Butter And Live Longer!
### How to Live off the Fat of the Land and Feel Great.

Americans are being saturated with anti-cholesterol propaganda. If you watch very much television, you're probably one of the millions of Americans who now has a terminal case of cholesterol phobia. The propaganda is relentless and is often designed to produce fear and loathing of this worst of all food contaminants. You never hear the food propagandists bragging about their product being fluoride-free or aluminum-free, two of our truly serious food-additive problems. But cholesterol, an essential nutrient, not proven to be harmful in any quantity, is constantly pilloried as a menace to your health. If you don't use corn oil, Fleischmann's margarine, and Egg Beaters, you're going straight to atherosclerosis hell with stroke, heart attack, and premature aging -- and so are your our kids. Never feel guilty about what you eat again!

Dr. Douglass shows you why red meat, eggs, and dairy products aren't the dietary demons we're told they are. But beware: This scientifically sound report goes against all the "common wisdom" about the foods you should eat. Read with an open mind.

**Rhino Publishing, S.A.**
**www.rhinopublish.com**

### The Joy of Mature Sex
### and How to Be a Better Lover

Humans are very confused about what makes good sex. But I believe humans have more to offer each other than this total licentiousness common among animals. We're talking about mature sex. The kind of sex that made this country great.

### Stop Aging or Slow the Process
### How Exercise With Oxygen Therapy
### (EWOT) Can Help

EWOT (pronounced ee-watt) stands for Exercise With Oxygen Therapy. This method of prolonging your life is so simple and you can do it at home at a minimal cost. When your cells don't get enough oxygen, they degenerate and die and so you degenerate and die. It's as simple as that.

### Hormone Replacement Therapies:
### Astonishing Results For Men And Women

It is accurate to say that when the endocrine glands start to fail, you start to die. We are facing a sea change in longevity and health in the elderly. Now, with the proper supplemental hormones, we can slow the aging process and, in many cases, reverse some of the signs and symptoms of aging.

### Add 10 Years to Your Life
### With some "best of" Dr. Douglass' writings.

To add ten years to your life, you need to have the right attitude about health and an understanding of the health industry and what it's feeding you. Following the established line on many health issues could make you very sick or worse! Achieve dynamic health with this collection of some of the "best of" Dr. Douglass'

**Rhino Publishing, S.A.**
**www.rhinopublish.com**

# PAINFUL DILEMMA

## Are we fighting the wrong war?

We are spending millions on the war against drugs while we
should be fighting the war against pain with those drugs!

As you will read in this book, the war on drugs was lost a long time ago and,
when it comes to the war against pain, pain is winning! An article in USA Today
(11/20/02) reveals that dying patients are not getting relief from pain. It seems
the doctors are torn between fear of the government, certainly justified, and a
clinging to old and out dated ideas about pain, which is NOT justified.

A group called Last Acts, a coalition of health-care groups, has released a very
discouraging study of all 50 states that nearly half of the 1.6 million Americans
living in nursing homes suffer from untreated pain. They said that life was being
extended but it amounted to little more than "extended pain and suffering."

This book offers insight into the history of pain treatment and the current failed
philosophies of contemporary medicine. Plus it describes some of today's most
advanced treatments for alleviating certain kinds of pain. This book is not another
"self-help" book touting home remedies; rather, Painful Dilemma: Patients in
Pain -- People in Prison, takes a hard look at where we've gone wrong and what
we (you) can do to help a loved one who is living with chronic pain.

The second half of this book is a must read if you value your freedom. We now
have the ridiculous and tragic situation of people
in pain living in a government-created hell by
restriction of narcotics and people in prison for
trying to bring pain relief by the selling of
narcotics to the suffering. The end result of the
"war on drugs" has been to create the greatest
and most destructive cartel in history, so great,
in fact, that the drug Mafia now controls most
of the world economy.

# Live the Adventure!

Why would anyone in their right mind put everything they own in storage and move to Russia, of all places?! But when maverick physician Bill Douglass left a profitable medical practice in a peaceful mountaintop town to pursue "pure medical truth".... none of us who know him well was really surprised.

After All, anyone who's braved the outermost reaches of darkest Africa, the mean streets of Johannesburg and New York, and even a trip to Washington to testify before the Senate, wouldn't bat and eye at ducking behind the Iron Curtain for a little medical reconnaissance!

Enjoy this imaginative, funny, dedicated man's tales of wonder and woe as he treks through a year in St. Petersburg, working on a cure for the world's killer diseases. We promise --

YOU WON'T BE BORED!

**Rhino Publishing, S.A.**
**www.rhinopublish.com**

# THE SMOKER'S PARADOX
# THE HEALTH BENEFITS OF TOBACCO!

The benefits of smoking tobacco have been common knowledge for centuries. From sharpening mental acuity to maintaining optimal weight, the relatively small risks of smoking have always been outweighed by the substantial improvement to mental and physical health. Hysterical attacks on tobacco notwithstanding, smokers always weigh the good against the bad and puff away or quit according to their personal preferences. Now the same anti-tobacco enterprise that has spent billions demonizing the pleasure of smoking is providing additional reasons to smoke. Alzheimer's, Parkinson's, Tourette's Syndrome, even schizophrenia and cocaine addiction are disorders that are alleviated by tobacco. Add in the still inconclusive indication that tobacco helps to prevent colon and prostate cancer and the endorsement for smoking tobacco by the medical establishment is good news for smokers and non-smokers alike. Of course the revelation that tobacco is good for you is ruined by the pharmaceutical industry's plan to substitute the natural and relatively inexpensive tobacco plant with their overpriced and ineffective nicotine substitutions. Still, when all is said and done, the positive revelations regarding tobacco are very good reasons indeed to keep lighting those cigars - but only 4 a day!

*Rhino Publishing, S.A.*
*www.rhinopublish.com*

### Bad Medicine
### How Individuals Get Killed By Bad Medicine.

Do you really need that new prescription or that overnight stay in the hospital? In this report, Dr. Douglass reveals the common medical practices and misconceptions endangering your health. Best of all, he tells you the pointed (but very revealing!) questions your doctor prays you never ask. Interesting medical facts about popular remedies are revealed.

### Dangerous Legal Drugs
### The Poisons in Your Medicine Chest.

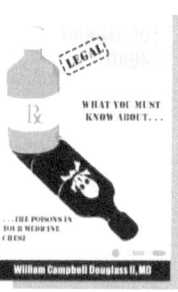

If you knew what we know about the most popular prescription and over-the-counter drugs, you'd be sick. That's why Dr. Douglass wrote this shocking report about the poisons in your medicine chest. He gives you the low-down on different categories of drugs. Everything from painkillers and cold remedies to tranquilizers and powerful cancer drugs.

---

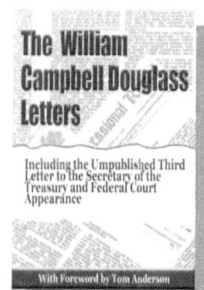

### The William Campbell Douglass Letters.
### Expose of Government Machinations
### (Vietnam War).

THE WILLIAM CAMPBELL DOUGLASS LETTERS. Dr. Douglass' Defense in 1968 Tax Case and Expose of Government Machinations during the Vietnam War.

### The Eagle's Feather. A Novel of
### International Political Intrigue.

Although The Eagle's Feather is a work of fiction set in the 1970's, it is built, as with most fiction, on a framework of plausibility and background information. This is a fiction book that could not have been written were it not for various ominous aspects, which pose a clear and present danger to the security of the United States.

### Rhino Publishing, S.A.
### www.rhinopublish.com

# I WANT TO GIVE YOU A FREE DAILY DOSE OF THE STRAIGHT SCOOP ABOUT HEALTH, MEDICINE, AND POLITICS

Join me as I journey far and wide exposing junk medicine, flawed science, vegetarian propaganda, FDA misinformation, big-government waste and fraud, and the antics of medical miscreants everywhere.

With my *Daily Dose*, you'll have the perfect companion to my newsletter—a continuous supply of urgent and timely health information like:

➤ The latest medical research—*without the PC spin*

➤ All the best natural cures—especially the ones *the drug giants want to keep quiet*

➤ The truth about diet, nutrition and weight loss—*without the sprouts and tofu*

➤ What your government has in store for you—and how *your rights are at stake*

All it takes is a second of your time to get yourself 'in the loop' by signing up for this invaluable FREE health resource. And I promise, I won't allow anyone else access to your e-mail address for any reason —I simply have too much respect for the privacy of my readers to allow it.

Just visit my website at **www.douglassreport.com** and give us your email address and I'll start sending you my *Daily Dose* immediately.

# HAD ENOUGH?!

## Everywhere you turn today, everyone keeps hollering at you:

"You're not eating enough VEGETABLES!"
"You're not getting enough EXERCISE"
"Give up MEAT! Give up COFFEE!"
"Get out of the SUN!"
"And while you're at it, GIVE UP
EVERYTHING else you love!"

## Nag, nag, nag! They never let up! But I've got great news...

My Dear Besieged Friend:

Everyone else is giving up coffee, alcohol, meat, eggs, fatty foods, sunshine and all things that make life livable. And then they're exercising like maniacs, sweating like horses and scolding YOU for not joining them. But you don't have to submit to this self-denial because...

*It's just JUNK MEDICINE.* It may look like the real thing, but when you see what it actually does to you, you'll be appalled. While masses of people meekly submit to these pseudo-science SACRED COWS, not even your doctor dares to ask, "WHY? HOW COME? SAYS WHO?"

But we're going to ask all those questions and you're going to love the REAL ANSWERS.

### So who am I to be swinging this ax?

*I'm William Campbell Douglass, M.D.* I've been called "the conscience of modern medicine," and the National Health Federation voted me "Doctor of the Year." I've flown with US Navy crews as a Flight Surgeon. Saved lives as a long-time emergency physician. Battled malaria in bullet-torn regions of Central America. I've even been called before Congress (they never asked me back).

I've also been labeled a "maverick," and several less flattering names too, but hey, that's part of the territory. And friend, my territory is everywhere. *And if there's one undeniable medical fact I've learned* in 40 years of treating patients all

*(continued on next page...)*

over the world, it's that…

## THERE IS NO SUCH THING
## as an undeniable medical fact!

When you become a subscriber to my newsletter *The Douglass Report* you'll see medicine just doesn't work that way. You're not a number, you're a human being. The most unpredictable thing in creation. And your own road to good health can be easier, cheaper and far more pleasant than any health-nag would ever predict.

By eating REAL FOOD, taking a few (cheap!) supplements that make you STRONGER, and doing some shockingly PLEASURABLE things that "everyone knows" can't be healthy!

And, to keep you ahead of the HEALTH NAGS and on top of the best new breakthroughs in the months ahead—YOU'LL GET THE BEST MONEY-SAVING DEAL on my all-you-need-to-save-your-life newsletter, *The Douglass Report*. Trust me, this is not another of those boring, preachy, you-heard-it-all-before publications that send you to sleep after raking you over the coals…

*The Douglass Report* IS DIFFERENT. I reveal the ridiculous truths about the latest JUNK MEDICINE MYTHS and hand you amazingly EASY AND PLEASANT new ways to free yourself and your loved ones from pain and disease.

Will you please let me put the power of all these health breakthroughs into your hands right now? Don't let self-righteous health sadists nag you to death…

---

Subscribe to *The Douglass Report* today! Call **1-800-682-6619**
and give the operator order ID# MRHBJ801.

---

Let me show you how shockingly pleasant the road to good health can be. If you do, I promise you'll feel illness, pain and weakness fade away like a bad dream. You'll see!

Sincerely,

*W. C. Douglass*

William Campbell Douglass II, M.D.
Editor

P.S. - Plus you have my Ultimate Guarantee that *The Douglass Report* will deliver all you're hoping for and more. Or else please, feel free to call off the deal. You get all your money back. Any time. For any reason. Period. So call and order your no-risk subscription today!

---

www.ingramcontent.com/pod-product-compliance
Lightning Source LLC
Chambersburg PA
CBHW020326130626
46549CB00003B/1046